# The
# Snake River
# CHALLENGE

Cover Illustration by Margarita Sikorskaia

Softcover ISBN 13: 978-1-7327646-1-3
Hardcover ISBN 13: 978-1-7346743-1-6

Printed in the United States of America

Cover and interior design by James Monroe Design, LLC.

Lucky Luke, LLC.
4335 Matthew Court
Eagan, Minnesota  55123

**www.KevinLovegreen.com**
Quantity discounts available!

# Chapter 1

My eyes pop open, and a smile hits my face. I quickly sit up in this unfamiliar bed. My own bed with my favorite soft blue comforter with airplanes on it is a thousand miles away.

Pale light sneaks into this little one-bedroom cabin. That tells me morning is trying to show itself. I look out the window to see the beautiful South Fork of the Snake River racing by only a short distance away. The soft morning fog floating above the surface of the water tells me it's chilly out there. It seems surprising—after all, it's July. But the weather is probably different out here in the mountains than home in Minnesota.

I look over to my right at the bed a few feet away. There's a lump in it, but there's no visible sign of my older sister, Crystal, or her long red hair.

My dad, Crystal, and I all have red hair, which is kind of cool. Mom has dark brown hair. Sometimes people joke with her, wondering if she's really our mom.

Crystal loves to sleep. She won't like getting up this early. But it's time to get going. This Idaho fly-fishing adventure is ready to begin.

Fly-fishing is so different than "regular" fishing, like we do in Minnesota for walleye, northern, and bass. Fly-fishing uses special rods, lures, and techniques. Instead of jigging for walleye, I'll learn how to softly cast a fly—which is a lure that really looks like a bug. With any luck, the colorful trout living in this cold river will see the fly floating downstream and *bam*! The fight is on! I can't wait to learn how to fly-fish!

Mom and Dad have been coming here to the Lodge at Palisades Creek for their annual fly-fishing trip for as long as I remember. My dad's cousin Justin has been running the lodge for years. This is the first time Mom and Dad have brought us along for their Snake River adventure. Maybe they feel we're old enough now that Crystal is fifteen and I'm thirteen.

We're the luckiest kids on earth that our parents share their love of the outdoors with us. Mom enjoys fishing, hiking, and spending time with us at our cabin back in Minnesota. Dad loves all hunting and fishing, and he does a great job showing Crystal and me the ropes.

I might be the only one who has more energy and excitement for hunting and fishing than Dad. And I usually have the best luck. That's why they call me Lucky Luke.

The Lodge at Palisades Creek looks like a little village to me. From the appearance of this place, I can picture a group of settlers living here a hundred years ago. And now, *we're* here, and Crystal and I get to go fly-fishing for the first time.

The main lodge building has a small restaurant, a gathering space with a big rock fireplace, and some old leather couches perfect for hanging out. Settled among the trees around the property is a handful of small log cabins.

There's also an awesome fly-fishing shop filled with cool stuff. It has a million flies for fishing. They're made with real feathers from pheasants, turkeys, peacocks, and other birds. The feathers make the lures look like a real bug to trick the fish. The shop is also filled with wooden-handled nets, sunglasses, hats, and shirts. There's a bunch of mounted trout hanging on the walls too.

When we first arrived at the lodge last night, I couldn't help but stare at those trout with their speckled, colorful bodies. They fill me with wonder. I can't wait to catch something so colorful and cool looking. This will be awesome!

But first . . . I need to wake up the sleeping lump in the other bed!

"Crystal . . . Hey, Crystal—it's time to get up." I do my best to keep my voice from scaring her out of her deep sleep. I carefully pad around the fluffy comforter until I find what I think is her head. "Crystal. It's time to get up."

"Mmmm. Whaaat? It can't be morning already," Crystal mumbles from somewhere under the sheets.

"It is, and it's beautiful outside. C'mon— we have to get up and get going. We gotta go wake Mom and Dad, eat breakfast, then go meet our fishing guides. This will be an amazing day!" I can hardly contain myself.

"What time is it?" Crystal asks as her mass of snarled red hair slowly emerges. It looks like a bird's nest covering her face.

I glance at the red glowing numbers of the clock on the nightstand. "Six thirty-six!" I proudly say.

"No way are you waking me this early, Luke. Go wake up Mom and Dad, and leave me alone."

She slides back under the sheets and disappears like an alligator slipping under the water. I guess that's what you can expect from a fifteen-year-old girl!

Giving up on her, I rummage through my duffel bag and find my clothes. I put on the supercool fly-fishing shirt Justin gave me last night. The material is really lightweight and smooth. It's tan with a patch from the lodge on the chest. It has big pockets on the front, where I can stash a box of flies or other fishing gear. The most important thing about the shirt is that it makes me feel like a real fly fisherman.

For now, I put my new polarized sunglasses in there. They are extremely cool, and Justin says they will help me see the fish under the water. I can't wait to see how they work.

I tiptoe over to the old wooden door and slip on my shoes. As soon as I pull the door open and step outside, the cool morning air sinks deep into my soul. I quickly realize I should have grabbed a light jacket. But I'm too excited to turn back—it's time to get going!

I scoot down the dirt path to the little log cabin right next to ours. I lightly knock and then creak the door open.

"Morning, buddy," Mom whispers, still snuggled in bed next to Dad.

From the soft snoring, I can tell Dad is doing what Crystal is probably back to doing in our cabin.

"Good morning! Aren't you guys ready to get some breakfast?" I say in a quiet voice out of respect for my still-snoring dad.

"Looks like someone's excited to go fishing," Mom says.

"That's for sure! C'mon—let's get going!"

Dad's snoring stops, but his head doesn't rise from his pillow.

"How about you run up to the main lodge and get your dad a cup of coffee? By the time you get back, we'll be ready to go," Mom says, finally sitting up.

"I'm on it. Back in a jiffy!" Out the door and on my mission I go.

# Chapter 2

After Dad's coffee and much pleading to get Crystal out of bed, we're finally ready for breakfast. We settle into the big wooden chairs at the restaurant. The staff serves us an amazing batch of pancakes that fill our entire plates. There isn't even room left for our bacon, so they serve that on an extra plate. I don't care which plate the bacon is on—the smell makes my mouth water either way.

While we eat, Justin arrives. He goes from table to table, greeting everyone. In addition to us, there are ten other people in the restaurant. He says hi to each guest. It sounds like he's making sure they're enjoying their stay.

Justin is a super nice guy. I can see he really cares about his guests. His tangled black hair sticks out of his charcoal-colored fly-fishing visor, which is peppered with a bunch of flies. Justin seems to be about the same age as my mom and dad. He's one of those guys who's always smiling, quick to laugh, and always on the move. Dad tells me Justin has been a fishing guide for the last seventeen years. It would be awesome to learn from him.

"Well, good morning," Justin says to us with a friendly smile. "You guys look like you're ready for a day on the river."

"Oh, we are," I reply.

"Crystal, are *you* ready?" Justin asks. He crinkles his eyes at her. She's probably not the first sleepy teenager he's seen at the lodge.

"A little more sleep wouldn't have hurt," she says, "but I'm ready to give this fly-fishing thing a shot." She smiles, trying to perk up.

"That's great—you're going to have a blast! You just wait and see. I'm so excited that all you guys are here," Justin says, attempting to pump some energy into this early morning. "I'll be even more excited after I get a cup of coffee. As soon as you're done with breakfast, meet me in the fly shop, and we'll get ready to go."

"Oh, are *you* taking us out?" Dad asks. He sounds surprised.

From what Dad had explained to us earlier, two of the guides who work for Justin would be the ones taking us out on the river. We didn't expect Justin himself to come out with us!

"Yep," Justin says. "I'm coming—and our awesome new guide Josh is coming too. I wouldn't miss it for anything."

"Awesome!" Dad says. "It's our lucky day. We get not only the best guide but the boss as well." He smiles.

Once we finish up breakfast, we head to the fly shop. We all go through the process of filling out our fishing licenses, which takes a little longer than I like. But as a bonus, we each get a cool metal water bottle with the lodge logo on it.

Finally, we head down the road to the boat launch. Mom, Crystal, and I get in Justin's black Ford pickup, and I get to be in the front seat. That makes me feel pretty cool.

Justin's pickup is awesome. He's proud that it has over 210,000 miles on it. The two cracks in the windshield add to the look, and Justin has a story for every fly stuck to the ceiling. It's far from clean, but I get the feeling the trucks out here are used for working. The guides don't seem too worried about how clean they look.

Dad is with Josh behind us. Justin tells us that Josh is one of the newest guides at the lodge. He has a master's degree, but he can't stay away from the river. He was born and raised in the area and knows the river like the back of his hand.

Josh has a sweet, jacked-up red pickup truck. At least, I'm pretty sure it's red under all those layers of dust. His gray boat bounces behind his truck on a little trailer.

"Why do you guys use these strange-looking boats out here?" I have to ask, since they're different than anything I've ever seen.

"Well, drift boats were invented just for the rivers," Justin says. "The shape of the boat helps it stay straight as it goes down the river. The flat bottom makes it easy for the rower to turn. And the seats and casting supports make it comfortable for the fishermen. It's a good way to go down the river in style and cover a bunch of water."

I nod with a proud smile. I like the idea of going down the river in style!

"When we use the drift boats, we have a huge advantage over wade fishermen," Justin continues. "Wade fishermen wear chest waders and walk in the water. They're stuck to one spot on the river, and we cover about five miles in a day. How many more fish do you think we go by?"

"A bunch," I say.

Justin's face fills with a big smile. Then he slowly turns and looks at me and says "Oh yeah!" in a deep, funny voice.

I look back at Crystal. Her lit-up eyes and big smile remind me of Christmas morning. She's definitely wide awake now. Mom just smiles and slowly shakes her head. I get the feeling she's watched Justin fire people up before.

"One thing you guys probably don't know," Justin says, "is that this river has three different trout species. Cutthroat, brown, and rainbow trout. That's one more thing that makes this river so special. I hope you guys catch one of each."

"Sounds like a Snake River Challenge," I say, putting my fist toward Justin.

"I like that!" Justin bumps my fist. His wide smile and bouncing head match his statement.

We arrive at the launch, where the boats go into the water. Both Justin and Josh get right to work. It's clearly not their first time doing this.

First, they pull out the fly rods, which are in two pieces. When stuck together, they're about twice the size of me. Each one slides into a rod holder that's part of the inside of the boat. I think it's a pretty good use of space.

I study every inch of the boat. Its anchor is square and about the size of a coffee can—clearly different than any anchor I've seen at home. It's hooked on a rope that goes off the back of the boat. The two big oars are slid into their spots, which are round metal circles on the sides of the boat.

There are three seats in each boat. That means two of us go with Justin, and the other two go with Josh. We decide that Mom and Crystal will go with Josh, and Dad and I will go with Justin.

"Later on," Dad says, "maybe we can switch up our teams."

Crystal, Mom, and I all smile and nod at that idea.

I'm pumped to fish with Dad—we're going to have a blast together. Not that I have any issue fishing with Mom. From hearing all the stories and seeing the pictures from Mom and Dad's annual fly-fishing trips, there's no question Mom loves fly-fishing. And from what Dad and Justin say, Mom is really good at it.

As Mom and Crystal settle in Josh's boat, Justin makes a grand gesture, as if welcoming me to his boat.

"Come aboard, sir," he says in a funny voice. "You can take the front seat. I'll sit in the middle so I can row and keep the boat the perfect distance from the shore. That way, you can cast from the front, and your dad can cast from the back."

Justin holds the boat steady as I climb in. Then, he carefully makes his way to the middle seat while crawling over a cooler and some tackle bags. Last but not least, Dad pushes us out onto the water, then hops in the back seat.

Off we go!

# Chapter 3

The current quickly moves us downriver. I can see the rocks on the bottom through the crystal-clear water. I figure it's deep enough to be just over my head.

The view downstream is amazing. I can't believe how beautiful everything is. There are spots where the cliffs reach high in the sky and overlook the river. And there are places where the trees and rolling hills sprawl out. The river is fairly wide and has big, gradual curves, kind of like a giant snake. I wonder if that has anything to do with the river's name.

Justin rows us over to a calm spot and drops the anchor *kerplunk* into the river.

"OK, Luke," he says to me. "Now we'll go through some fly-casting basics."

Dad settles in to watch Justin do his magic and explain the art of fly-fishing.

Justin pulls out the really long rod with a strange reel on the end. There's one fly about two inches long tied to the fishing line. A smaller fly is tied on about a foot below the big fly.

"We'll start out with an ant and a dropper rig,"  Justin explains. "The big ant will float on top. That's basically your bobber. The tiny fly is the dropper. That's what most fish will bite on. We're starting with a dropper called a pheasant tail nymph."

Justin shows me the tiny fly. It has a gold bead head, bright-green body, and shiny gold tinsel wrapped around it. The

 tail is made of two small red feathers sticking out. It looks like a tasty bug for a hungry trout!

"Now, here's how you cast," Justin says.

I listen intently, trying to soak it all up.

He points the rod away from the boat. I notice the reel is facing down, just like the reel on the spinning rod I use for walleye.

"You pull some line out with your left hand because we right-handers hold the rod with our right hands," Justin explains. "Put your thumb on top, resting it on the cork and pointing it down the middle of the rod. Then move the rod back and forth over your right shoulder."

He moves the rod just as he describes it. He pulls out more line with his left hand to get some distance.

# Imaginary Clock

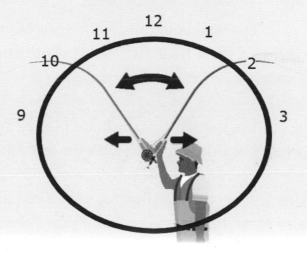

"Imagine a clock," he says. "When the rod is pointing straight up, it's at twelve o'clock. So then when you send the line behind you, be sure to stop at two o'clock. Then drive the rod forward, propelling the line, and stop at ten o'clock. It's OK to say 'ten and two' out loud as you're casting." He leans closer to me. "But use your inside voice so you don't totally drive your dad nuts."

I laugh.

"The goal is to roll the line out on the water and get it to lie flat," Justin continues. "Be patient—it'll take some practice."

Justin starts driving his arm back and forth as he pulls line out with his left hand. He's smooth, and the line stays well above us. After a few back-and-forths, which he calls false casts, he hits the brakes at ten o'clock.

The forward momentum sends the two flies through the air. They roll out perfectly on the water and land near the bank. I can tell that's exactly where Justin wants them. He lets them float downstream for a second or two. Then he pulls some line in with his left hand and repeats the cast. It looks easy.

Sort of.

Justin turns to me so I can see how he's holding the rod. "Luke, do you see how I'm keeping the line up high at twelve o'clock when I cast?"

"Yep."

"That's the goal. If you keep the line up high, I won't have to pull any hooks out of your hat. Or, more importantly, my hat." Justin smiles with his eyes wide open to make his point. "The next thing I want to show you is called a mend," he says. "This is very important, and you'll do this on almost every cast."

I'm staring at his hat, but then I snap back to attention. This is like being in school—I realize I have so much to learn. I feel a little nervous about remembering all these instructions.

"As soon as your fly hits the water near the bank, you want to make sure the fly is leading the way down the river. If the line leads the way, it tends to drag the fly. And fish don't like to see the line dragging the fly."

I try not to laugh. It sounds like he just said, "Fish don't like to see *dragonflies*."

"The mend is when you pick up your rod tip and make a rainbow motion back upstream with your fly line. The goal is not to move the fly when you do it. The ultimate goal with fly-fishing is to get the fly, or flies, to float naturally. That way, the fish think they're real. The mend is the best way to cause this to happen. Got it?"

"Got it," I say brightly, hoping to drum up some confidence.

"One more thing before we start fishing," he says. "When you're fishing back home in Minnesota, you know how to set the hook, right? Meaning, you jerk the line so the hook sinks into the fish's mouth."

"Yeah!" I say. I know exactly what he's talking about.

"Well, we do it a little differently out here. With a fly rod, you simply raise the rod tip, just like you're making a cast. You don't set the hook with a jerk, like you do for a largemouth bass at your grandparents' cabin in Minnesota. And the magic words are 'take it.' The moment you hear me say 'take it,' raise your rod tip as quick as you can. I'm here to help you, and I have a pretty good eye for seeing the fly get eaten by a trout."

Justin lets out a big breath and smiles at me. "Whew! That was a lot of information. Do you have any questions?"

He's right—it *is* a lot of information! But I'm here to have fun and do my best. I smile back at him.

"I don't have any questions right now," I reply. "I think I need to give it a try and see how it goes."

Justin nods at me proudly as he hands the rod over. "OK. Here you go. Let's have you make a couple of casts."

I try to remember it all: pull the line out, back-and-forth motion, twelve o'clock, ten and two . . . The first couple of casts are awkward. It's hard to get the fly to roll out.

"Try not using so much wrist," Justin coaches. "Keep your arm close to your side and your wrist locked. Let the rod do all the work. Another good thing is to picture smoke coming off the tip of the rod. You want to keep that smoke in a straight line above you, not in an arc."

The smoke idea is a cool tip. After a few tries, I slowly start getting the hang of it.

"You're right," I tell Justin. "This will definitely take some practice. But I'm up for the challenge. I want to catch some trout!"

With a satisfied nod, Justin hands Dad a rod, then pulls the anchor.

"What are we waiting for, then?" he says. "Let's do this!"

# Chapter 4

We drift downstream for a bit. Mom, Crystal, and Josh's boat floats just ahead of ours.

Before long, Justin taps me on the shoulder. "Get your flies in the water," he says with some fire. "This is a great bank that holds some awesome brown, cutthroat, and rainbow trout."

Dad and I quickly stand up and get ready.

"Fish on!" Dad yells like a sergeant, pointing downriver with his rod.

"Put your legs in between the casting supports," Justin directs. "That will keep you from falling out of the boat if I hit a rock or the boat shifts."

I lean into the supports, steady myself, and attempt my first cast. The line goes out only about ten feet and slaps the water. The harder I try, the more the line slaps.

"OK, Luke. Relax, slow down, and let the tip of the rod stop at ten o'clock," Justin coaches.

I take a deep breath and calm down. On the next cast, I slow the rod speed down and stop at ten o'clock. Like magic, the fly line rolls out and lands softly on the water.

"There you go—just like that," Justin says. He rows backward to slow the boat down.

I beam. I did it!

I look over at Dad to see if he noticed my great cast. But instead, I'm surprised to see his rod bent way over with the tip going crazy.

Justin sees it too. "Yeah, baby! Good job, cuz! Give me a second, and I'll pull over to that calm water. Then you can bring him to me," Justin says with excitement.

Justin eases us over to the bank as Dad plays the fish. Breathlessly, I watch Dad bring the fighting trout to the side of the boat. Justin drops anchor, then pulls out his net and scoops up the trout.

"Oh yes! A huge brown trout to start the day," Justin says.

"That could be one of my biggest ever!" Dad beams at the fish.

Justin carefully unhooks the brown trout and hands it to my dad.

"What do you think, Luke? It's a beauty, isn't it?" Dad says with a giant grin on his face.

"Yes, sir!" I exclaim. "That's a good one."

"About twenty inches?" Dad asks Justin.

"I'd say more like twenty-two, but who's measuring?" Justin says with a laugh. "Let's get him back in the water and keep him healthy."

Dad carefully slides the fish back
in the water. Instantly, the fish shoots off
into the middle of the river. Dad and Justin

high-five. Then Justin grabs the anchor rope lying between his feet, pulls the anchor back up, and rows us back out into the current.

"Your turn, Luke. Let's get you on the board," Justin says.

I'm totally pumped up after seeing Dad's fish. Now I'm so excited to catch my first fish too. I hurry to get my fly to the bank. Of course, that just makes the line and the two flies slap the water again.

"Slow down, Luke," Justin says with an easy voice. "Remember what you did last time—you've got this."

I take a deep breath and slow down the cast. I finally lay a perfect cast next to the bank.

Just then, Dad yells out again.

"Yeah, baby—got him!"

I look back to see Dad pulling in another one. I quickly start reeling in my line to get out of Dad's way. But then my line drifts back and wraps around Justin's oar. Instantly, it's all wrapped up.

"Oh no!" I groan.

"Just leave it, Luke," Justin says with a little laugh. "I'll deal with that in a second."

Frustrated, I sit down in my seat. Here I am, trying so hard to cast, trying so hard to catch a fish. Meanwhile, Dad's already on his second. And on top of that, my line is all tangled up.

Dad quickly brings in another trout. Justin doesn't miss a beat. He scoops it up in the net and hands the fish back to Dad.

This trout is much smaller than the first one. Honestly, that makes me feel a little better.

"I'm gonna have you deal with the fish," Justin says to Dad. Then Justin turns to me. "Now, Luke—let's get you untangled and back in action."

I'm surprised Justin stays so calm. He doesn't seem mad that I'm tangled up. He simply stops rowing and lets the boat drift. He pulls up the oar and skillfully unwraps my line. Apparently, this isn't the first time he's done it.

"You're good to go!" Justin says, tossing both flies back into the water.

I race into action, hoping to beat Dad to the next fish. I quickly pull out some line and begin to do the back-and-forth motion.

Just when I figure I have enough line out to make it to the bank, Justin gives me the signal to let it go.

I stop at ten o'clock, and the fly lands one foot from the bank.

"Oh, that's a nice one! Now throw a mend in it," Justin says quickly.

I move the rod in a rainbow arc. The line flips over, just as it's supposed to.

"Nice job!" Justin says. "Keep your eye on the top fly. Any twitch at all, raise the tip."

I stare at the fly as it races down the bank.

Then I hear Justin yell, "Take it! Take it!"

I quickly raise the tip, just as he told me. But nothing's there.

"What happened?" I ask. "I didn't feel anything."

"You had a taker," Justin explains, "but you missed him. You were just a little slow on the set. That allowed the tiny hook to slide out of the trout's mouth. But that's all right. You'll get this figured out!"

I roll the fly right back to the bank. Only this time, it rolls a little too far . . . Then it gets caught in the grass.

"Uh-oh! Give it a pull, give it a pull," Justin says with urgency.

I pull, but the line doesn't budge. Meanwhile, the current keeps pulling us downriver—farther and farther away from my flies. Justin starts rowing back upstream as hard as he can. I give a few more hard pulls. But it's clear the river will win this battle.

"Point your rod tip right at the flies and hold the line tight," Justin tells me.

I do as he says. The line quickly builds tension. Gritting my teeth and giving a frustrated growl, I squeeze the rod with both hands so it won't fly out of my grasp. Suddenly, the line snaps and launches over our heads. Dad ducks to avoid getting hit. The line is loose—but the flies are long gone. They're still stuck back in the grass.

"It's all good," Justin says quietly, his head down. "But those were my two best flies . . ."

"*What*?" I look at Justin quickly.

Both Dad and Justin burst out laughing.

"I'm just kidding!" Justin says, giving my shoulder a squeeze. "I have a bunch more where those came from. But you should've seen your face. You had that look like you just broke your grandma's best plate."

I sit down in my seat, feeling frustrated again and now defeated. I can't catch a fish. I can't cast. And now I can't even keep the flies on my line.

Justin rows over to calm water near the bank and drops the anchor. He grabs my line and ties on two new flies.

"This is fly-fishing, Luke," Justin says. "It happens all the time."

"Yeah," Dad chimes in. "If you're not catching the bank once in a while, you're probably not casting close enough. Isn't that right, cuz?" he asks Justin.

"That's correct!" Justin answers.

Like flicking a light switch, I instantly feel better. I smile at Justin as he hands me my line with the new flies.

"Thanks! That was fast," I tell him.

He sends me a proud wink. "Now let's hook one!"

We resume floating down the river. I stand up, lean into the casting supports, and get ready for action. With new determination, I launch my flies at the bank.

"Perfect!" Justin says. "Great cast. Now mend and let it go."

I mend, and the fly floats with purpose down the bank. Then I see it. The ant twitches, just like a bobber does when I fish at our lake cabin.

Quick as a rattlesnake, I raise the rod tip.

"Boom!" I yell. "Got him!"

My rod bends, and a jolt of excitement races through my whole body. I can feel the power of the fish fighting against my line.

Justin immediately heads for the calm of the shore. "Keep your tip up. You're doing great."

I can barely breathe as I fight the fish. I reel and reel, pulling the fish closer and closer, until I can finally see it next to the boat. The gold colors flash in the water.

"A beautiful brownie," Justin says.

He eases the net into the water and scoops up the trout.

"Yes!" I yell.

I can't believe it—my first trout! Justin pops out the hook and hands me the fish.

"See? This is easy, isn't it?" Dad jokes.

"Picture time," Justin says, pulling out his cell phone.

"Good call!" Dad says, pulling out his phone too.

Justin and Dad both take pictures of me and my first trout. I bet my smile is as wide as the trout is long.

This trout is smoother than any fish I've ever felt. It's super slippery and hard to hold. It slides through my hands and lands in my lap. I pick it up with a firm grip, yet I'm careful not to hurt the fish.

Suddenly, I remember Mom and Crystal in the other boat. I've been so focused on fishing—I totally forgot they've been here this whole time too.

"Hey!" I call over to them. I proudly raise the fish up high. "My first trout!"

Mom, Crystal, and even Josh hoot and holler for me.

"All right," Justin says. "Time to get him back in the water."

"Oh! Right!" I say. I lean over, ease the fish back into the ice-cold water, and watch it race away.

"Nice job, Luke. That's how you do it," Dad says. "How fun was that?"

"Amazing!"

"Way to go, Luke!" Mom says as their boat floats by us.

I give her a thumbs-up and a proud smile.

"Got him!" Crystal suddenly shouts.

We all watch and cheer as she pulls up her rod and fights a fish like she knows what she's doing.

"Is that your first one too?" I ask excitedly.

"No!" she shouts back with a laugh. "I've been pulling 'em in left and right!"

Her funny smile and the way she looks at Josh tell another story. Everyone—myself included—laughs with her.

"A rainbow!" Josh yells over as he scoops up her catch.

"Nice, Crystal! That's awesome!" Justin yells back.

Everyone is super excited. Especially me, now that I've finally caught my first fish.

This is really fun!

# Chapter 5

"Fish on!" Dad calls out again.

Justin and Josh give each other a salute, and then both boats continue downriver.

Now that I'm in the game, Dad and I can work our casts at the same time. Even though I'm in the front of the boat and Dad is in the back, it still takes careful effort to keep our flies out of the other's way. Each time my fly lands somewhere in the middle, Justin reminds me to cast it in front. There's a lot to keep track of, but it's a blast!

All the while, Justin calls out signals to me. He tells me to aim right in front of that big rock or next to that log. He's doing everything he can to get me a fish, other than cast my rod himself.

"Boom!" I yell.

"Oh my!" Justin yells at the same time.

We both see a fish swim up and attack my ant. Its whole mouth comes out of the water. I can't believe how cool it is. I lift my rod tip and feel the weight of the fish on the other end.

"Oh, Luke! That's a pig!" Justin's voice vibrates with excitement. "Keep your rod up, and I'll row us into the calm water. Hang tight. Oh my goodness—he's huge!"

Justin can't keep calm. Neither can I. I'm breathing hard and almost whistling through my tight lips. The fish is pulling hard, so I let line slip through my pointer finger—just like Justin taught me. This reel isn't the same as the kind I'm used to. With the fly-fishing reel, you control the line with your pointer finger. When the slack is all out, the reel takes over.

Now Dad and Justin are both coaching me.

"Let him take the line out," Justin suggests.

"Take your time with this guy," Dad adds.

I can't stop grinding my teeth as the fish tugs. I slowly pull in line as I hold my rod up high. Suddenly, the monster jumps out of the water right next to the boat.

"Oh man!" Justin and Dad yell at the same time.

"It's a huge brown trout!" Justin barks.

"Come on, Luke—get him in. You have to get your hands on this guy," Dad says.

It's hilarious. I haven't seen Dad this excited since I shot my twenty-five-pound turkey. I have to get this trout in the net.

Finally, the fish settles down, and I gain on him. I pull and pull until Justin reaches way into the water, arm and all, and scoops up the fish.

"Yeah!" Justin yells, holding the net high.

"Woo-hoo!" Dad cheers.

Justin lowers the net back in the water to keep the fish healthy. Then he grabs his pliers and pops the big hook out of the side of the fish's mouth.

"Perfect hook job," Justin says as he hands me the fish.

Once again, Dad and Justin snap a couple of pictures.

"Put him back in the net," Justin instructs. "Let's give him a breath of air and then measure him."

I place the trout back into the net, which Justin has already lowered into the ice-cold water. It makes me laugh a bit to remember that's how fish get a "breath of air." Then Justin pulls him back into the boat. He carefully sets the big brown on the inside ledge of the boat and measures its length.

"Nineteen inches!" Justin boasts.

"Nice!" Dad says.

Justin eases the fish back into the net, then lowers it into the water again. The amazing fish swims away to fight again another day.

"Now that's as good as it gets," Justin says. He sits back in his seat and shakes his head. "You the man, Luke!"

"Thanks! That was awesome!" I reply. "Did you see how he came up and attacked the ant?"

"I did. It's great when they eat the top fly like that," Justin says.

We continue to drift down the river, working the bank. Like clockwork, Dad and I catch several other fish.

From the other boat, Mom and Crystal wave us over. As we get closer, they keep pointing into the thick brush along the bank. Josh puts his hands over his head, imitating antlers.

We ease in next to them. Then we see it. A giant bull moose is standing just off the bank. His dark-chocolate fur is on the edge of being black. His eyes carefully watch us as we slowly drift closer. He doesn't seem scared at all. I'm sure a drift boat with three people in it is almost as common as a bird flying by for this guy.

"There's a cow moose too," Crystal whispers, pointing.

I don't see anything at first, but I look again. Sure enough, there's a cow standing behind a big bush.

Everyone sits quietly and watches the moose for a while. Then it seems they've had enough of us. The moose, with their crazy long legs, trot up the grassy hill and disappear over the top.

"That was fun to see," Justin says.

"Yes, it was," Mom agrees. "By the way, how're my boys doing over there, Justin? They aren't getting too excited or anything, are they?"

"Oh, Sue, you know them too well. No one's jumped out of the boat after a fish yet, but it's come close a couple of times," Justin says with a laugh. "I love their excitement. It makes fishing fun!"

"You know . . ." Dad begins. He gazes up at the sky, using his hand to shield his eyes. "That sun sure looks like it's directly overhead . . ."

Crystal and I look up at the sun too. It makes us squint. What in the world is Dad talking about?

But Mom just sighs and shakes her head. "You know what that means," she says to Justin.

He nods and laughs. "Lunchtime!"

# Chapter 6

We float around the next corner and pull over for lunch. This back channel of the river is calm, clear, and shallow. The shore is covered with a million smooth round gray rocks, each about the size of a grapefruit. The boat clunks when we hit shore.

I can't help but think what an amazing morning it's been. Everyone caught fish, and the weather has been perfect—nice, warm, and not a cloud in the sky.

Josh, Crystal, and Mom pull up close enough that our oars touch. It almost looks like the boats give each other a "side five." Suddenly, I'm right next to Mom.

"Howdy, stranger," I say in my best cowboy voice.

"Howdy back, not-so-stranger," Mom replies.

"Let's enjoy our lunch aboard ship, shall we?" Justin says in his funny voice.

He digs into the cooler and pulls out two lunchboxes. He hands one to Dad and one to me.

I do a double take. Mine is a metal Spider-Man lunchbox—one that would make a first grader proud. The tin is cold from being tucked inside the cooler. I flip the latch with my thumb and peek inside. It's full of good stuff: a turkey sandwich, a small bag of BBQ potato chips, a perfectly red apple, and one big chocolate chip cookie! I instantly realize how hungry I am.

"Thanks! This looks great!" I say.

"You're welcome," Justin says without looking back. "We have to keep you fueled up so you can handle all this hard work."

He's busy digging into the cooler for his own lunchbox. He finally pulls it out, and I see Wonder Woman is on it. I bet Crystal would love that one.

I look over at the other boat. "What lunchboxes do you guys have?" I ask.

"I have the Hulk, Mom has Iron Man, and Josh has Captain America," Crystal reports.

"That's a pretty good showing of superheroes," I add. "How about you, Dad?" I ask next.

"Clearly not the right one," Justin says with a smirk.

It's a Superman lunchbox.

"Actually, mine fits me perfectly," Dad says. "I've been doing a lot of push-ups lately!"

"You wouldn't believe the jokes and stories that get brought up when these lunchboxes come out," Justin says through a mouthful of sandwich. "It works every time."

We take a much-needed rest and eat our lunches. It's peaceful here with only the sound of the river rolling by. Dad eventually crawls out of the boat, finds a grassy spot, and plops down on his back.

"There he goes," Mom says.

"He sure does like his naps, doesn't he," Crystal comments.

"He's been doing that since we were kids," Justin says. "He goes a hundred miles per hour, then his batteries need to be recharged."

"You got that right," Mom says, smiling.

"Say," Justin remarks, looking at me then Crystal. "Do you guys know the South Fork of the Snake River starts in Yellowstone National Park as the Snake River?"

"I don't know anything about this river," Crystal says.

"Nope, me either," I add.

"Well, here's a little history lesson for you," Justin continues. "It flows out of Yellowstone Park through Jackson Hole, Wyoming, then into Idaho's Palisades Reservoir. The reservoir is like a huge man-made lake. This river is home to twenty-four bald eagle nests, which is the largest concentration of nests outside of Yellowstone. In this area, it's common to see moose, deer, elk, bald eagles, golden eagles, and lots of ospreys and hawks."

"Cool!" Crystal and I say at the same time.

Justin nods. "And the native fish in the river is the Yellowstone cutthroat trout.

We haven't caught one in our boat yet." He turns to Josh. "How about you guys?"

"Not yet," Josh says with a grin, "but these gals are sure trying!"

"Cutties, as we call them, are a beautiful species found only in the western United States," Justin continues. "They like to eat insects floating on the surface of the water. Fishermen refer to these bugs as 'dry flies.' No species of fish eats dry flies better than Yellowstone cutthroat trout. That's why we love to fish them."

Justin pauses for a second. "We do have a big problem, though. Yellowstone cutthroat trout live in only sixty percent of their original habitat. Climate change, pressure from invasive species, and competition from non-native trout, like rainbows, are affecting their population. Do you like the metal water bottle we gave you this morning?" he adds, surprising us.

"Yeah, they're super cool." Crystal holds hers up proudly. "I love the colorful sticker with the lodge logo on it."

Justin points at her bottle. "Last year we started giving each of our guests one of those water bottles. Before that, we just used plastic water bottles. But can you believe that we used to go through about four thousand plastic water bottles each summer? All that waste! Now, you get to take the water bottle home with you to remember us and your adventure. How cool is that! Using metal water bottles is one of many things the lodge does to help the trout in our small way. This river, the trout in it, and the animals and birds that live here are very special to those of us who call this place home. And we love sharing it with special guests like you guys."

Mom smiles. "Thank you, Justin," she says. "I always learn something new from you when we visit."

"And as a new guide," Josh adds, "I learn a lot from guys like Justin, who've lived here a long time."

"Just doing what I can!" Justin replies with a laugh. "Well, what do you guys say? Should we get back out there?"

"Yeah!" I exclaim.

Justin gathers up the lunchboxes and tucks them back into the cooler.

"Before we go, let's change up your flies."

First, he grabs Dad's flies and snips the line just above the big ant. He carefully tucks the two flies into one of his many tackle bags. Then, he opens a green plastic container full of flies of all colors and sizes, and he carefully picks out the perfect fly. He looks like he's an insect professor.

The whole time, I keep a close eye on what he's doing so I can learn a few tricks.

Next, he artfully ties a knot like a surgeon and pulls it snug to the big fly. Then he stretches out about two feet of clear line from a small round plastic holder. He looks over his shoulder at me.

"This is called tippet. It comes in many strengths, and it's crystal clear. The goal is to use a tippet with the smallest diameter so the fish don't see it. But it also has to be strong enough so it doesn't break. Number one is the really heavy stuff. I'm putting on a number four."

The numbers mean nothing to me. I'm just glad Justin knows what he's doing.

He ties the tippet to the hook of the big fly and ties another small fly onto the other end.

"Remember, the small fly is called the dropper," he explains again. "OK, now hand me your line, Luke."

Again, like a surgeon, he snips off my flies and ties on new ones. His fingers work like magic with those tiny flies and the light tippet.

When he hands the line back to me, I carefully check out the flies. The big one looks just like a grasshopper, wings and all. The tiny one's supercool. It has a gold bead head, with a purple flash on its back, and the body is black with a tiny feather tail.

"All right—the sun is at the perfect angle," Justin says, lining his thumb up to the sun.

Crystal and I look at each other, cocking our heads. I get the feeling she isn't buying this either.

Justin notices Crystal's expression out of the corner of his eye. He looks right at her with a very serious glare.

Playing into Justin's game, Crystal quickly flashes back to a normal face.

"How dare you question my sun-gauging abilities! This is serious stuff," Justin says matter-of-factly.

But the smirk at the end of his stare tells a different story. We all start laughing.

Justin is hilarious. Dad once told us that Justin takes after his dad, Uncle Don. From what I hear, it's constant laughs between the two of them.

"OK, gang—let's get moving. We have a long way to go," Justin says. "Sue, how about you hop in our boat and join Team Lucky Luke? You guys said you want to switch up the teams, right?"

"Sounds good to me," Mom says. She turns to Josh and smiles. "Thank you for all your help. You're excellent at what you do!"

I give Mom a hand as she climbs into our boat. Justin guides her past him until she's finally settled in the back seat, where Dad used to be. Mom hands Dad's backpack to Crystal.

"Come on, Dad. It's time to go!" Crystal yells. For the record, it's not quite as gentle as the voice I used to wake her up this morning.

Dad's head pops up from the grass like he got poked.

"Luke, give us a shove-off please," Justin says.

I hop out of the boat. Leaning into it, I push as hard as I can. Like a walrus, the boat slides off the rocks and back into the water. I take one step into the water before I jump back into the boat.

"Whoa! The water's freezing cold!" I say, plopping down onto my seat. I turn my foot so the water runs out of my sandal.

"Trout love that cold water," Justin explains. "That's what keeps the fish strong and healthy in this amazing river."

"Make sure to show your dad how it's done, Crystal!" Mom calls over as we start to drift out. "Enjoy your time together."

Crystal gives us a slow thumbs-up. She cocks her head and flashes a proud smile. "Oh, I will," she says.

"She's a funny one, that Crystal," Justin says, laughing.

"Hey!" Dad calls out. "The boat that brings in the most trout before the takeout wins the Snake River Challenge!"

"What do we win?" I call back.

"The losers buy ice cream on the way back!" Dad says.

"You're on!" I say confidently. "C'mon, Mom—we can do this."

"I'll see what I can do," she replies. She smiles and shakes her head.

"And for the record, we already have a Snake River Challenge going. Right, Justin?"

I say. "The original challenge was to try to catch all three kinds of trout."

"Looks like we have two of them going now," he says with a wink.

# Chapter 7

Picking up my fly rod, I'm ready for action. I can't wait to catch another trout and win some ice cream. What a bonus!

"All right, you guys," Justin says with fire in his eyes. "It's usually not about how many fish you catch but the experience you have on the adventure. But . . . I don't like losing to your dad, so I'll make an exception today. Let's get serious!"

Mom and I lay our flies right off the bank on many casts. But the fish seem to be napping or something. We struggle to get even a bite.

Then we hear Dad whooping it up. They definitely have a fish in their boat.

"Be patient, guys," Justin says. "The fish don't eat all day. They eat when the hatch happens."

"The hatch?" I repeat.

"When the temperatures change throughout the day, different bugs hatch from the water," Justin says. "The baby bugs—the larvae—are usually attached to rocks on the bottom of the river. After they hatch, they float or swim to the surface. When they hit the surface, they spread their wings and fly away. Many times, they float on the water for a while to dry out their wings. The fish will either eat the bugs as they rise from the bottom or sip them off the top."

I had no idea that bugs came from the river—I'm not sure where I thought they came from. But now that I think about it, I realize that most of the time I'm by water, especially toward evening, there are a bunch of bugs around. In Minnesota, it's usually mosquitoes.

"Throughout the year," Justin continues, "different bugs hatch at different times. My job is to figure out what kind of bug is around at any given time and match the fly on your line. Our goal as guides is to learn the patterns. And trust me, it takes a long time to figure it out. Most of the guides talk after each day on the river to learn from one another. We especially try to help the new guides figure things out. That is, if they're willing to listen to us old guys!"

"Well, Josh must be one of those willing to listen," Mom says, "because he's a great guide."

"Over the last couple of days, in the afternoon, the grasshoppers have been very active," Justin says. "That means we'll put our flies right on the banks. The trout will think a grasshopper fell in. And *bam!*— they'll eat it."

It's incredible how much Justin knows about the river, its bugs, and how to catch fish at any time. He sure knows a lot after being out here for seventeen years.

"Oh, there we go," Mom says calmly as she keeps her rod tip high.

I can't believe it—she's got a fish, and yet she's so calm! Though, by the look of her smile, she's clearly enjoying the fight. Me, I'd yell so loud the eagles sitting in the trees would fly away.

"Good job, Mom!"

She pulls in a nice trout, and Justin scoops it up.

"Woo!" I do the shouting for Mom.

I try to be loud enough so the other team knows we have a fish in our boat. Dad and Crystal both look over. Justin holds up the net for proof.

"At last! A beautiful Yellowstone cutthroat trout," Justin says. "Remember—this is our prized catch, and no doubt, that's why our best fisher put the first one in our boat."

"Ha!" Mom says with a humble smile.

"And we just accomplished Luke's version of the Snake River Challenge! We caught all three trout species in the river— rainbow, brown, and cutthroat," Justin says proudly.

"How can you tell it's a cutthroat?" I ask.

"See the red lines under its lower jaw?"

"Yep," I reply.

"Those are the markings of a cutty."

After a quick picture of Mom with her fish, she slides it back into the water. Justin and Mom high-five.

"Hey, look over there," Justin says. He points across the river.

I turn my head and see a doe and fawn drinking from the river. The deer don't seem to mind us one bit. The little one has a spotted coat. It's cool—we've seen moose and now deer!

As we continue downriver, I see some huge cliffs ahead. They're on both sides of the river, and the water is pinched in between.

"The canyon section is coming up," Justin says with a little more volume. His eyes light up. "This will be good. I heard from some guides this morning that the fish have been biting like crazy in there."

"Cool. I'm ready!" I say with wild eyes and a big smile. Justin's excitement is contagious.

"You better be," Justin says. "The water will be rolling fast. You need to keep your balance and land your flies tight against the cliff. Giant fish hang out in the fast, deep water—and when you hook one, you'll be in for the fight of your life!"

# Chapter 8

The cliffs on each side of the river tower above us. The rock walls look jagged, layered, and smooth all at the same time. If the sun weren't directly above, the canyon would probably be completely shaded inside.

Justin starts calling out signals. "Bounce your flies right off the cliff edge. Or under an overhang, if there is one."

Mom and I are doing our best, but it's a bit of a challenge. The water is a little faster in here, and there are some wavy spots where huge boulders must be underneath. The rapid current makes it harder to keep my balance using the casting supports. I'm trying so hard to get my fly right in "the zone," as Justin calls it. And then I have to quickly mend my line so the fly will float naturally for a second or two. It's tricky.

But then—as if it were magic—a gigantic mouth comes out of the depths and swallows my big grasshopper. I pull up the rod just as a big wave hits the boat. The force makes me fall back and land in my seat. I'm still holding my rod up, though, so the fight is on!

From all the ruckus I'm making, Justin and Mom realize I have a fish. But Justin can't help me at all. Instead, he's focusing all his efforts on keeping the boat upright in the waves.

"Play her out until we get through this rough section," Justin demands.

"Her? Why do you say her?" I ask through clenched teeth.

"All the big fish are females. And this seems like a big one!" Justin says with a smile as he bucks back and forth with the waves.

Mom reels in her line and watches me fight the fish. My line is slipping fast through my fingers.

"Hold her tight," Justin says quickly. "Don't let that monster get out in the middle."

I squeeze my fingers and hold on with all my might as the rod tip is forced down. It feels like it's attached to the back of a car.

"Guide her back toward the cliff— keep your rod tip up," Justin barks out.

I grit my teeth as I pull my rod tip up and to the left. The fish actually follows my lead and slowly heads back toward the rock wall. She lets me bring in some line.

As soon as we shoot out of the fast run, Justin rows us over to the side where the water is calmer. My line is pointing straight down now. The fish feels like a giant lead weight on the other end. I feel her massive strength each time she pushes through the water. I fight with all I have until my rod is up high again. Then I pull in line and ease the rod back down. I feel like I'm reeling in a whale.

"You're doing great, bud—you got this," Mom says. She smiles at Justin.

I get the feeling they both know this is a special moment with a really big fish. It's a team effort now, and I want to land this baby for all of us.

I keep the pressure on. Just when I think I'm about to see her colors in the water, she takes off like a rocket ship out of control. I have to let the line zip through my fingers because I don't want the tippet to break.

"Oh, good job! Keep letting her run, Luke!" Justin urges.

As my right arm starts to burn and tire out, I finally see a flash of gold.

"She's getting tired. You almost have her, Luke," Justin says, calmly now.

I ease her straight up and finally can see her whole body. She's a giant! Without a word, Justin puts the net in the water up to his armpit. I guide the giant toward the net.

Justin grunts as he scoops in the fish. He quickly pulls the net, the fish, and plenty of water into the boat.

"Woo! *Yesssss*!" he screams out.

"Oh, Luke, that's a fantastic fish," Mom says. "Way to go!"

Justin quickly lays the amazing brown trout on the boat ledge and measures it.

"Twenty-one inches long!" Justin barks out. "A true trophy!"

I carefully hold the fish with both hands as Mom and Justin snap pictures. I can't contain the smile on my face. This is so cool!

I slide the fish back in the net, and Justin eases it into the water. He lets the giant trout hang out for a moment and then pulls the net away. The trout slowly swims out of sight—but it will stay locked in my memory forever.

"That's one of the coolest things I've ever done," I say, sitting back in my chair. I'm totally exhausted.

"Well, get ready to do it again! There are more sections just like that one coming up," Justin says. He tilts his head down, looking over his sunglasses at me. "And, by the way, that makes two fish in our boat."

Mom and I start casting our flies toward the bank. But Justin tells us not to waste our energy—the good spot is coming up. We both sit down and hold our flies in our hands so they don't get tangled up. After a short drift, Justin tells us to get ready. Like soldiers manning our posts, we lean into our casting supports. Both Mom and I are excited for more action.

"Now!" Justin commands.

We each make a couple false casts and then let our flies go. We're next to another cliff wall that just *has* to hold fish.

I look back and see Mom drop her fly right next to the wall. She mends like a pro, and the fly floats aimlessly along the edge.

"Nice cast, Mom!" I can't keep my eye off her fly. It looks like a perfect float.

In that moment, we all see a huge mouth come up and eat Mom's fly. At the same time, Justin and I yell out, "Oh!"

Mom sets the hook and grips the rod with white knuckles. "Oh my, this is a big fish," she says.

Again, Mom fights the fish and never once yells out. It just isn't her style. Instead, she smiles and shakes her head whenever the big fish takes out her line. The whole time, I bite my lip to keep from hooting and hollering. I'm going crazy inside!

After several minutes of epic fighting, the fish finally gives in. Mom eases the fish into Justin's waiting net. When he lifts up a giant brown trout, he and I do enough yelling for Mom. We make sure Dad and Crystal can hear us. We're pumped. It's another amazing trout!

Justin quickly sets it on the ledge and measures the trout.

"My goodness, guys. It's twenty-two inches long. This is the biggest fish I've netted this year. Good job, Sue—you're awesome!"

"Way to go, Mom!"

"Thanks, guys," she says, as calm as ever. "That was really fun. And my biggest fish ever. I clearly needed the luck of Mr. Lucky Luke in the boat with me."

Just then, I look up and spot one of the biggest golden eagles I've ever seen. It flies right over us.

"Look at that," I say, pointing up.

"It's definitely an amazing day," Mom says with a peaceful smile. "That might just be your grandpa's spirit keeping an eye on you."

A smile grows on my face while I picture my grandpa. He would have loved being here, catching fish like this.

Then suddenly, it's as if someone turned down the lights in the canyon. I feel the temperature drop.

"Oh no," Justin says with a frown.

It catches me off guard.

"We're in for some weather," he says, pointing at the darkening sky above. "And that looks like a doozy."

# Chapter 9

Justin waves to the other boat. After a sharp whistle, he gets Josh's attention. Josh rows down to us.

"We need to get off the river—*now*," Justin says, immediately taking charge. "We'll have to see what happens with this storm."

Justin and Josh row fast downriver. The rest of us quickly dig through our packs for our rain jackets.

I look with wide eyes at Justin. His face relaxes just a bit.

"This happens all the time out here," he explains. "One minute we have blue skies, and the next minute wind and rain. Don't worry—we're not far from a spot that will give us some shelter."

I nod, knowing we're in good hands.

Justin guides the boat onto the bank as the wind begins to howl like a fierce cat. Mom holds the boat while Justin and I pile out. Instantly, the rain starts falling from the dark sky. The drops are so big they hurt my face.

We all hurry up the bank and tuck under a huge rock overhang. There's just enough room for all six of us to huddle underneath.

Then the loudest thunder crack I've ever heard rings out. It echoes through the canyon. I flinch, and Mom wraps her arms around me.

"It's going to be all right. Storms move through quick," Justin says. He almost has to yell so we can hear him over the deafening rain.

At that moment, lightning shoots across the sky. For a second, it lights up the river. But then everything goes dark again. Thunder cracks a second later.

The sheets of rain are relentless. I can't even see the boats right in front of us. But then the lightning flashes again, and there they are. More thunder follows.

It's like we're caught in a movie. We sit helpless for several minutes, just staring out at the rain. There's nothing we can do and nowhere to go. We're at the storm's mercy. I'm very thankful for this huge rock.

Sheets and sheets of rain race down the river. I'm afraid the boats will be filled to the top once it ends—*if* it ends. I close my eyes and say a quick prayer. I figure it can't hurt. I open my eyes and continue to watch the fury of lightning, thunder, and endless rain.

But before too long, I realize it's getting quieter. I can see a ray of light fighting its way through the black clouds. And then, across the river and over the steep rock ledge, a line of blue sky races behind the clouds.

"Almost over!" Justin says. He doesn't have to yell now.

The quieter it gets, the calmer I feel.

"That was crazy," Crystal says, looking with wild eyes at Mom and me.

I take a big breath and let it out fast. "Yes!"

"Five more minutes and the sun will be out, and we'll be back on the river," Justin says. He pokes Dad on the shoulder. "By the way, we have three fish in our boat. Victory of the Snake River Challenge is looking good for us."

I get the feeling Justin is trying to reel us back in and put the storm behind us. It's working. Just hearing him talk about fish makes me feel better.

"Well," Dad begins, "we have two fish so far. And I haven't lost faith in Crystal."

As Justin predicted, within five minutes the sky is blue, and a huge rainbow fills the sky.

"Check that out," I say. "I hope that means there's a huge rainbow trout at the other end."

"Wouldn't that be nice!" Crystal adds. "Can you believe how fun it is catching these trout?

"They're unbelievable. I can't wait to get out there and catch another one," I say. I nudge Mom with my hip to get her moving.

We crawl out from the overhang and march single file over to the boats. We have to bail out water with a red plastic cup. It takes a little extra time, but it's worth not having to stand in water while we fish. Soon we're back in fishing mode, heading down the river again.

There's no sitting down for the rest of the float. Mom and I work the fly rods like we're pros. We catch three more giant brown trout, one really nice rainbow, and three Yellowstone cutties. It's one of the best fishing days of my life. From what we can hear coming out of the other boat, Dad and Crystal are doing well too.

I realize this might be the most excited I've ever seen Mom, which is pretty cool. And the scenery on the river is something I'll never forget—the cliffs, the eagles, the sparkling water.

"There's our takeout," Justin says.

I look up and see the dock just downriver. Even after a whole day of catching fish, I'm not ready to stop. I desperately send my flies toward the bank, hoping for one more fish.

"How many fish are you guys up to?" I yell over to Dad.

"Ten! How about you guys?"

"Ten!" I yell back. I turn to Mom. "Come on, Mom—we have to get one more. We can't end in a tie!"

"I'm content, Luke. It's all up to you," she says, smiling. Then she sighs and looks at Justin. "Does he sound like anyone you know?"

"The apple doesn't fall far from the tree," Justin says with a big smile.

"I'm going for it!" I exclaim. I pull my flies close and get ready to cast one last time.

"If you get a fish now, it's all up to you to get it in," Justin tells me. "I have to make sure we make it to that dock. One thing we can't do is miss the takeout. But keep fishing—there are plenty of fish here!"

I think he realizes there's no way I'm stopping now.

Mom reels in her flies and sits down. She seems amused just watching me.

I look in front of the boat for the best spot to send a cast. I finally let the flies loose.

The dock is getting closer and closer with every second. Time is running out. We *can't* end in a tie!

I hold my breath as I watch my flies drift along the bank. And then it happens—a giant mouth comes up and swallows the grasshopper.

"Boom! Got him!" I yell.

"Nice!" Justin says. "You have what we call a takeout fish. The last fish of the day!"

He pulls us up to the dock while I fight the beauty in.

Justin hands me the net to scoop up the fish—a Yellowstone cutthroat!

"A nice cutty to end the day," he says.

I unhook the fish and hold it up for Dad and Crystal to see as they pull in next to us. Dad pretends to look mad, but I can see how proud he is.

"That's number eleven!" I say. I give the fish a kiss before sliding it back into the clear water.

"Now *that's* how you end an amazing day and win the Snake River Challenge!" Dad says. He reaches out, and we shake hands.

"Thank you! And I'll take chocolate!" I can't wait to taste that ice cream.

We all laugh as we climb out of the boats. On the dock, I pause for a moment, turn around, and look at the river.

This has been one of the most exciting fishing days of my life. I think about the river, the fish, and the challenge of putting the flies in the right spot. It's been awesome to spend time with Mom, Dad, and Crystal on this amazing adventure. I will cherish the memories and pictures forever.

We took on the Snake River Challenge—and the way I see it, we're all winners!

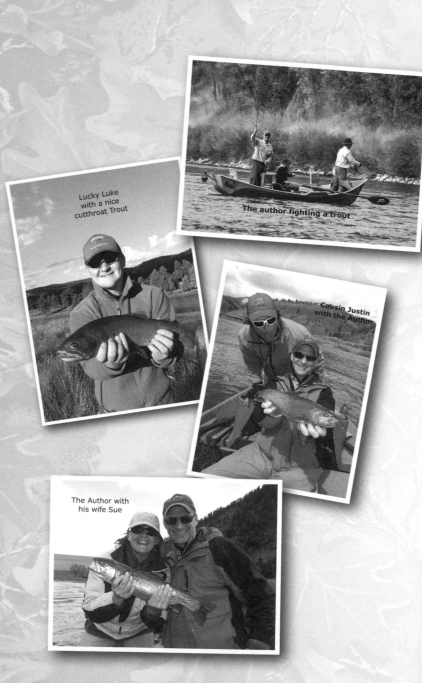

Lucky Luke with a nice cutthroat Trout

The author fighting a trout

Cousin Justin with the Author

The Author with his wife Sue

# About the Author

Kevin Lovegreen was born, raised, and lives in Minnesota with his loving wife and two amazing children. Hunting, fishing, and the outdoors have always been a big part of his life. From chasing squirrels as a child to chasing elk as an adult, Kevin loves the thrill of hunting. But even more, he loves telling the stories of the adventure. Presenting at schools and connecting with kids about the outdoors is one of his favorite things to do.

Monster Mule Deer

Lucky Luke's
25lb. turkey

The
Muddy
Elk

Crystal'
1st buc

Lucky Luke
with a large
mouth bass

Lucky Luke's
1st bear

Crystal, The Swamp hero!

**www.KevinLovegreen.com**

# Other books in the series

To order books or learn about
school visits please go to:
**www.KevinLovegreen.com**

All the stories in the Lucky Luke's Hunting Adventures series are based on real experiences that happened to me or my family.

If you like the book, please help spread the word by telling all your friends!

Thanks for reading!
Kevin Lovegreen